The Best NFL
Quarterbacks of All Time

© 2025 ReferencePoint Press, Inc.
Printed in the United States

For more information, contact:
ReferencePoint Press, Inc.
PO Box 27779
San Diego, CA 92198
www.ReferencePointPress.com

ALL RIGHTS RESERVED.
No part of this work covered by the copyright hereon may be reproduced or used in any form or by any means—graphic, electronic, or mechanical, including photocopying, recording, taping, web distribution, or information storage retrieval systems—without the written permission of the publisher.

LIBRARY OF CONGRESS CATALOGING-IN-PUBLICATION DATA

Names: Roland, James, author.
Title: The best NFL quarterbacks of all time / by James Roland.
Description: San Diego, CA : ReferencePoint Press, 2024. | Includes
   bibliographical references and index.
Identifiers: LCCN 2024039650 (print) | LCCN 2024039651 (ebook) | ISBN
   9781678210045 (library binding) | ISBN 9781678210052 (ebook)
Subjects: LCSH: Quarterbacks (Football)--United States--Biography--Juvenile
   literature. | Football players--United States--Biography--Juvenile literature.
Classification: LCC GV939.A1 .R648 2025 (print) | LCC GV939.A1 (ebook) |
   DDC 796.332092/2--dc23/eng/20241007
LC record available at https://lccn.loc.gov/2024039650
LC ebook record available at https://lccn.loc.gov/2024039651

Introduction 4
Passing into History

Chapter One 8
Johnny Unitas: The Golden Arm

Chapter Two 16
Roger Staubach: Captain America

Chapter Three 24
Joe Montana: Joe Cool

Chapter Four 32
John Elway: Bronco for Life

Chapter Five 40
Tom Brady: The GOAT

Chapter Six 48
Patrick Mahomes: The King of Kansas City

Source Notes	56
For Further Research	59
Index	61
Picture Credits	64
About the Author	64

Passing into History

By the time Peyton Manning was ready to start his fifteenth season in the National Football League (NFL), he had already put together a career worthy of the Pro Football Hall of Fame. He had won a Super Bowl and four league Most Valuable Player (MVP) awards, while racking up records for passing yards and touchdowns. But the Denver Broncos quarterback was about to rewrite the record book again.

In the very first game of the 2013 season, against the defending Super Bowl champion Baltimore Ravens, Manning threw for seven touchdown passes—the most by any quarterback in one game since 1969. And he never slowed down or looked back. When the season was finished, Manning had set the single-season records for passing yards (5,477) and touchdowns (fifty-five). And the Broncos as a team broke the single-season scoring record with 606 points in sixteen games. "Peyton was on fire everywhere, we felt it in practice, we felt it in the meeting rooms and most importantly, we felt it in games,"[1] linebacker Von Miller, Manning's former teammate, told ESPN in 2023.

Manning's understanding of the offensive game plan and what defenses would try to do to stop it was legendary. He also excelled at getting the ball to his receivers, whether they were open or not. These qualities put him in a rarified group: one of the greatest NFL quarterbacks of all time. These quarterbacks were not just great passers, they were creative, being able to make big plays when it seemed like things were falling apart. They were leaders, able to rally their teammates to victories in the face of defeat.

The It Factor

Former New Orleans Saints quarterback Drew Brees, another record-breaking superstar, said the all-time great quarterbacks also have a winning quality that is hard to define, but fans and teammates can sense it. "All the successful ones have the 'it' factor, a certain charisma about them," he told NFL.com. "When it comes to how you play the game, they throw with great accuracy, great anticipation. There's an ability to make clutch plays, an ability to make smart decisions, good decisions in critical situations."[2]

Way back in 1976, during Super Bowl X, Pittsburgh Steelers quarterback Terry Bradshaw made one of those smart decisions while his team was holding on to a slim two-point lead over the Dallas Cowboys late in the fourth quarter. Facing third down and four yards to go for a first down, and with the ball on Pittsburgh's

QUARTERBACK STATS

Peyton Manning earned five MVP awards in his career, more than any other player in NFL history.

thirty-six yard line, Bradshaw assumed Dallas would expect a short, safe pass. Instead, he told his main receiver, Lynn Swann, to run a deep post pattern (a long run down the middle of the field toward the other goal post). After receiving the snap from his center, Bradshaw dropped back to pass as two Cowboy defenders blitzed. Just as Dallas tackle Larry Cole crashed into Bradshaw, the Steelers Hall of Famer launched a perfect strike to Swann. Swann caught the ball in stride and raced into the end zone for a touchdown, effectively putting the game out of reach. NFL Films called Bradshaw's pass "the Greatest Throw of All Time."[3]

Measuring Greatness

Bradshaw completed only nine of nineteen passes for 209 yards that day. By comparison, in 2024, when Patrick Mahomes led the

Kansas City Chiefs to victory in Super Bowl LVIII, he completed thirty-four of forty-six passes for 333 yards. Football has changed in some important ways, with offenses relying mostly on the passing game and rule changes meant to protect quarterbacks and allow receivers to run downfield with less contact from defenders. As a result, the passing statistics of today's quarterbacks dwarf those of their predecessors.

Although passing and scoring stats certainly tell one part of a quarterback's story, other factors can be just as important in determining the greatest of all time. The best ever were leaders

At the Broncos' home field in Denver, Colorado, quarterback Peyton Manning warms up for a game against the Seattle Seahawks on August 18, 2012.

who made all their teammates better. They also rose to the occasion to pull out wins when losses seemed inevitable. As Bleacher Report sportswriter Nick Kostos writes,

> More than touchdowns or yardage, the most important characteristic I want in my quarterback is the ability to come from behind and perform well when it matters most. If the team is down by 13 with six minutes left and the ball, how much faith do you have in the quarterback to lead you to victory? To me, the greatest quarterbacks are able to overcome incredible odds and win games singlehandedly for their team.[4]

The list of quarterbacks who seemed to play at a level well above their peers is a short one. But when they did come along, they provided football fans countless thrills along the way.

Johnny Unitas: The Golden Arm

Johnny Unitas's football career did not take the path he had hoped for at the beginning. He did not play for his first-choice college, and he was cut by the NFL team that drafted him before he ever got to throw a pass in a regular-season game. But by the time he retired after a long and remarkable NFL career, he owned a collection of passing records and was well on his way to the Pro Football Hall of Fame.

Most of his career was spent with the Baltimore Colts, long before they moved to Indianapolis. In Baltimore, Unitas (nicknamed "Johnny U") helped popularize the NFL and became a hero to sports fans in Maryland and beyond. Famed *Sports Illustrated* writer Frank Deford, who grew up idolizing Unitas in Baltimore, once wrote, "Ultimately, you see, what he conveyed to his teammates and to Baltimore and to a wider world was the utter faith that he could do it. He could make it work. Somehow, he could win. He would win. It almost didn't matter when he actually couldn't. The point was that with Johnny U, it always seemed possible."[5]

The Long Road to Stardom

John Constantine Unitas was born in Pittsburgh in 1933, the third of four children born to Leon and Helen Unitas. His father died of kidney disease when Unitas was just five years old, and his mother worked two jobs to support the family. In high school, Unitas played quarterback and halfback.

Unitas grew up dreaming of playing for the University of Notre Dame, which consistently had one of the best college teams in the nation during the 1940s and 1950s. But Notre Dame's coach, Frank Leahy, told Unitas during a tryout that he was too skinny and would get hurt playing college football.

Unitas also tried to play for the University of Pittsburgh, but he failed an entrance exam, forcing him to try other colleges. Undeterred, Unitas eventually enrolled at the University of Louisville in Kentucky, where he played not only quarterback but also safety and linebacker on defense, and he returned kicks and punts on special teams. Although Unitas remains a Louisville legend, he actually had an unspectacular college career. His entry into the NFL was equally unremarkable. The Pittsburgh Steelers selected Unitas in the ninth round of the 1955 NFL Draft but cut him from the team before he ever got a chance to play.

By that point he had married his college sweetheart and needed a job to pay the bills. While he was working construction in Pittsburgh, some friends convinced Unitas to play for a semiprofessional football team called the Bloomfield Rams. He earned fifteen dollars a game.

In the summer of 1956, a year after being dropped from the Steelers, Unitas and his friend and Bloomfield teammate Jim Deglau borrowed some gas money and

A 1964 Philadelphia Gum football card features Baltimore Colts star quarterback Johnny Unitas.

drove to Baltimore to try out for the Colts. Unitas not only made the team but also became Baltimore's starter after quarterback George Shaw broke his leg early in the season.

The following year, Unitas led the NFL in passing yards and touchdown passes. He also led the Colts to a 7–5 record, the first winning season in franchise history. The legend of Johnny U was just beginning.

Unitas at the Helm

For most of the NFL's first four decades, the pro game had relatively few devoted followers. There was no Super Bowl, no ESPN, no internet to catch up on game highlights, and only a dozen teams in the league. But near the end of the 1950s, that began to change—mostly as the result of one big game starring Johnny Unitas. On December 28, 1958, in the bitter cold of Yankee Stadium in New York City, the 1958 NFL Championship Game pitted the New York Giants against the Baltimore Colts. The Giants dominated most of the game, but as the clock ran down to the final seconds, Baltimore quarterback Johnny Unitas led his team deep into New York territory. The Colts kicked a field goal to tie the game, forcing the first overtime game in NFL history.

Now in sudden death and with 45 million television viewers, the Giants could not make a first down on their first possession. Baltimore took the punt and then, with Unitas at the helm, marched eighty yards in thirteen plays to set up the game-winning touchdown. Unitas was named game MVP, and the thrilling contest became known in football circles as the greatest game the sport had ever seen, kicking off the rapid growth and popularity of the professional game. Within two years the rival American Football League (AFL) formed, and eventually the NFL and AFL decided to have

QUARTERBACK STATS

Between 1956 and 1960 Johnny Unitas threw at least one touchdown pass in forty-eight straight games—a record that stood for fifty-two years until it was broken by Saints quarterback Drew Brees in 2012.

10

Unitas Still a Part of Baltimore Football

Visitors entering M&T Bank Stadium, home of the Baltimore Ravens, must pass through a section that bears a familiar name to longtime football fans. Soon after Johnny Unitas died on October 4, 2002, the Ravens dedicated the main entrance area of their stadium as Unitas Plaza and unveiled a statue there of the football legend. Fans had petitioned the Ravens to name the entire stadium after Unitas, but the naming rights had already been leased to M&T Bank. However, just north of Baltimore, in Towson, Maryland, stands Johnny Unitas Stadium, a multiuse facility for Towson University's football team, men's and women's lacrosse teams, and other squads. It is also the site of Unitas's last public football pass—a toss he made when the stadium (then called Towson University Stadium) was re-opened after a renovation just weeks before the quarterback's death. The following year, the school renamed the stadium after Unitas. The honor was especially significant for his family, as three of Unitas's children had graduated from Towson University.

their champions play in a new contest called the Super Bowl. In the 1970 the leagues merged, and excitement for pro football took off around the country.

The 1958 NFL Championship was the first for Baltimore, who repeated the feat against the Giants the following season. Unitas led the NFL in passing yards, touchdown passes, and completions on his way to the 1959 MVP award. Within only a few years in the league, Unitas had earned the respect of some of football's all-time greats. Before the start of the 1960 season, Vince Lombardi, the legendary coach of the Green Bay Packers, said of Unitas and the Colts, "Without him, they're ordinary. With him, they're great. He's the best quarterback I've ever seen."[6]

More Records and Championships

Throughout the 1960s, Unitas continued his brilliant play. In 1960, he became the first quarterback to throw for more than three thousand yards in a season and led the NFL in touchdown passes for the fourth straight year. One of the secrets to his success:

he often waited until the last second to make sure his receiver would be open before launching a pass. This technique usually resulted in a first down or touchdown.

One of Unitas's favorite targets in those days was Colts wide receiver Raymond Berry. Berry once tried to describe what set Unitas apart from other quarterbacks of his era, saying it was Unitas's "uncanny instinct for calling the right play at the right time, his icy composure under fire, his fierce competitiveness, and his utter disregard for his own safety."[7]

Unitas won MVP awards again in 1964 and 1968, the same season he took the Colts all the way to another NFL Championship. But by then the NFL champions had started playing the AFL champions in the Super Bowl. Following a smashing 34–0 shutout of the Cleveland Browns in the 1969 NFL title game, the Colts prepared for the AFL champion New York Jets. Super Bowl III saw a major contrast between its quarterbacks. Johnny Unitas, with his crewcut and black leather high-tops, had a decidedly "old school" vibe compared to New York's flashy young Joe

Unitas looks to pass the ball during a 1967 game. Unitas's passing accuracy earned him NFL MVP awards in 1959, 1964, and 1968.

Namath, who had longer hair, sideburns, and no shortage of confidence. Namath famously guaranteed a victory prior to the game, which made headlines because players seldom taunted their opponents leading up to a big contest.

As it turns out, Namath's prediction came true, and the Colts lost their first Super Bowl game. Undeterred, Unitas and the Colts bounced back to reach Super Bowl V in 1971, this time winning the big game with a close 16–13 victory over the Dallas Cowboys.

> ## QUARTERBACK STATS
>
> Johnny Unitas led the NFL in passing four times (1957, 1959, 1960, and 1963). Only three other quarterbacks—Drew Brees, Sonny Jurgensen, and Dan Marino—have more seasons as the league's top passer.

Johnny U's Legacy

Super Bowl V proved to be the final high point for Unitas and the Colts. Under new ownership, Baltimore traded their star quarterback to the San Diego Chargers in January 1973. His 1973 season in San Diego was disappointing, as years of injuries finally caught up with the man once nicknamed "the Golden Arm."

Unitas retired prior to the 1974 season after becoming the first NFL quarterback to throw for more than forty thousand yards in a career and the first to throw for more than thirty touchdowns in a season (thirty-two in 1959). At the time of his retirement, he owned almost every passing record possible.

In his first year of eligibility, Unitas was elected to the Pro Football Hall of Fame. In his induction speech, Unitas focused more on his teammates and coaches than his own record-setting achievements. "A man never gets to this station in life without being helped, aided, shoved, pushed and prodded to do better," he said in his speech. "I want to be honest with you: The players I played with and the coaches I had . . . they are directly responsible for my being here. I want you all to remember that. I always will."[8]

Though his playing career ended in San Diego, Unitas happily returned to Baltimore in retirement to continue raising his family and begin the next phase of his life. Football fans soon found him calling NFL games on CBS. And whenever he could, Unitas joined former teammates and other buddies on the golf course.

Playing Through Pain

But playing golf and just performing everyday activities became tougher for Unitas as he got older. The brutal hits he took on the football field and the injuries to his knees, shoulders, elbows, and hands started to take their toll. His right hand, the one that had thrown game-winning touchdown passes for so many years, grew weaker and weaker due to nerve damage. Just to hold a golf club, Unitas had to take his left hand and wrap his right fingers around the club and keep them in place with a velcro strap. "I have no strength in the fingers," he said in a 2001 *Sports Illustrated* article about the long-term health struggles of NFL veterans. "I can't use a hammer or saw around the house. I can't button buttons."[9]

Unitas holds an ice pack to his knee after sustaining an injury on December 5, 1965. Frequent injuries took a heavy toll, causing health problems for Unitas later in life.

Iconic Sports Footwear:
Johnny Unitas's Black High-Tops

These days many sports superstars have signature sneakers and lucrative deals with companies like Nike and Adidas. But long before Michael Jordan's Air Jordan basketball shoes kicked off the sneakerhead revolution in the 1980s, Johnny Unitas was associated with his particular footwear. Throughout his career in Baltimore, Unitas wore simple black high-top cleats, unlike most NFL players, who preferred low-cut shoes. Unitas's shoes became such a part of his image that the Pro Football Hall of Fame displays the high-tops he wore during his last season as a Colt. For Unitas, the shoes were not really a fashion choice or an effort to be different. In a 1999 interview with NFL Films, Unitas said he liked the extra support the high-tops gave his ankles. "They were comfortable," Unitas said. "I saw no reason to change them. The only time I wore low-cuts was in college. I cracked an ankle (in a scrimmage). I started wearing high-tops because of the ankle." Today, you can find NFL players wearing high-tops as well as mid- and low-cut cleats. But no one yet has become linked so clearly with high-tops as Baltimore's Johnny U.

Quoted in Chris Willis, "Johnny Unitas Week: High-Top Cleats and Crewcut," *Pro Football Journal* (blog), May 6, 2016. www.nflfootballjournal.blogspot.com.

Despite the pain and discomfort he experienced later in life, Unitas used his popularity to raise awareness of the health problems experienced by so many former football players. He spoke out on behalf of retired players who had serious injuries and lobbied the NFL to provide better medical benefits for players in retirement.

Right up until his death in 2002, Unitas remained a popular and admired NFL star in retirement, just as he had been during his thrilling playing career. "Johnny Unitas will always be a legendary name in NFL history," NFL commissioner Paul Tagliabue said after Unitas's death. "One of the greatest quarterbacks to ever play the game, he epitomized the position with his leadership skills and his ability to perform under pressure."[10]

> **QUARTERBACK STATS**
>
> Johnny Unitas was selected to the Pro Bowl ten times between 1957 and 1967.

Roger Staubach: Captain America

As a young boy, Roger Staubach had two dreams: serving his country and becoming an NFL quarterback. He managed to do both. He served in the US Navy after graduating from the US Naval Academy in 1965 and became a Hall of Fame quarterback with the Dallas Cowboys after his naval obligations were fulfilled.

Staubach embodied many old-fashioned, all-American ideals in both his personal and professional life. He married his high school sweetheart, Marianne Hoobler, and they raised five children. He won the Heisman Trophy while playing for the Naval Academy and won two Super Bowls with the Cowboys. And long after he retired from the navy, Staubach volunteered on behalf of programs that helped veterans. In 2018 he received the Presidential Medal of Freedom—one of the highest honors given to civilians.

From Boy Scout to Heisman Winner

But Staubach's remarkable life started out in pretty simple surroundings in a little corner of southwest Ohio. Staubach was born in 1942 in Cincinnati, Ohio, and grew up in a small house in the nearby suburb of Silverton. His father was a traveling salesman, and his mother was a secretary with General Motors. Staubach was their only child, and they supported him in all of his childhood activities—from Boy

Scouts to youth sports. Until he started playing quarterback in high school, Staubach loved baseball more than anything and wanted to one day play for his hometown Cincinnati Reds.

As devout Catholics, Staubach's parents enrolled their son in Purcell High School, a Catholic high school in the East Walnut Hills neighborhood of Cincinnati. There Staubach excelled in three sports: basketball, baseball, and football. But it was not until his senior year that he started playing quarterback. Until then, he had been a decent, if not remarkable, wide receiver and defensive back.

Purcell's coach, Jim McCarthy, urged Staubach to consider playing quarterback. But the future Heisman Trophy–winning quarterback was not so sure.

> **QUARTERBACK STATS**
>
> Roger Staubach is one of only two quarterbacks to win a Heisman Trophy and a Super Bowl. He is also the only Heisman winner to appear in five Super Bowl games—the most ever.

"Switching positions probably changed my life," Staubach said in 2007. "I think I could have gone on to college and been an okay player as a receiver, but I don't think I would've had a professional career. I owe a lot to my coach who saw something in me that I didn't know was there. As quarterback, I discovered I liked leading the team, and that change had a major influence on my future."[11]

The switch to quarterback fit Staubach perfectly and put him on a path to becoming one of the nation's top college and professional quarterbacks in the years ahead. During his senior year of high school, Staubach was recruited to play quarterback for several major universities, but he decided to join the navy. He first attended the New Mexico Military Institute for a year before enrolling at the US Naval Academy in Annapolis, Maryland, where he also was a three-sport star.

Navy's 1963 season was remarkable, both for the team and for its star quarterback. In his junior year, Staubach led the Midshipmen to a 9–1 record, a number two ranking in the polls, and a berth in the Cotton Bowl, where he set bowl records for completions (twenty-one) and passing yards (228). The 1963 season was also special because Staubach won the Heisman Trophy—the award given to the top player in college football. In 2013, the fiftieth anniversary of his Heisman season, Staubach told ESPN why that award in particular is one of the most meaningful to him. "One of the reasons is that I've always looked at it as a team award, because if I don't have a really good team that year, I don't come close to winning the Heisman," he said. "That team was one of the most special teams I've ever been a part of, and we're still very close."[12]

The Long Detour to NFL Stardom

When Staubach graduated from the Naval Academy, it was 1965 and the Vietnam War had been raging for nearly a decade. Like all academy graduates, Staubach was required to serve at least four years as an officer in the US Navy or Marine Corps. Staubach, now an ensign in the Navy Supply Corps, volunteered for a one-year tour in Vietnam. He commanded forty enlisted sailors and supporting Navy SEALs and swift boat crews that patrolled the rivers and coastal waters of Vietnam. In a 1966 interview with the armed services newspaper *Stars & Stripes*, Staubach said his focus was on doing his job in Vietnam and getting back to his wife and baby daughter in Cincinnati. When asked about whether he missed football, Staubach answered, "Sure, I miss football, in fact, quite a bit. But I hope to get a chance to play [football] while in the Navy."[13]

Roger Staubach attended the United States Naval Academy, where he won the 1963 Heisman Trophy playing for the Midshipmen.

Staubach and the Original Hail Mary

Roger Staubach was raised Catholic and continued to practice his faith throughout his life. The Hail Mary is a traditional Catholic prayer often said when someone needs help. In a 1975 playoff game against Minnesota, with only seconds on the clock and his team down 14–10, Staubach launched a fifty-yard pass to receiver Drew Pearson. Pearson caught the pass and ran into the end zone for the winning touchdown. Staubach later told reporters he had said a Hail Mary when he threw the ball, and soon the term *Hail Mary pass* became used whenever a quarterback throws a long pass to the end zone with time running out.

Returning to the United States in 1967, Staubach got that chance as he continued his military career at Naval Air Station Pensacola in Florida. There he played quarterback on one of the station's football teams, the Goshawks. And after two years with the Goshawks, Staubach was ready for the big leagues.

The "Old" Rookie

The Dallas Cowboys had drafted Staubach in 1964 after his junior year at the Naval Academy, knowing that he would be unable to join the team until 1969—once his commitment to the navy was completed. Like a lot of teams, the Cowboys liked what they saw of Staubach's remarkable 1963 season and were willing to wait and take a chance on him down the road.

In the summer of 1969, Staubach resigned his naval commission just in time to join the Cowboys in training camp as a twenty-seven-year-old rookie ready to battle Craig Morton for the starting quarterback job. "Age is a factor. But if you can play at 21, you can play at 27," Staubach said in a 2012 interview. "I was in better shape at 27 than I was at 23."[14]

Staubach was a backup to Morton for two seasons, until he earned the starting job halfway through the 1971 season. He led

> **QUARTERBACK STATS**
>
> By the time he graduated in 1965, Roger Staubach had set twenty-eight Naval Academy records—all of the records a quarterback could hold.

Go, Go Goshawks!

To help stay in shape and keep his quarterback skills sharp during his four years in the navy, Roger Staubach ran and exercised and passed the football whenever he could. During his tour in Vietnam, Staubach ran on a soccer field near his base at the Chu Lai Port near Da Nang. When he arrived for his next tour of duty in Pensacola, Staubach finally got to put on football pads, a helmet, and a uniform for games against college football players. "I hadn't played for two years, but putting on the equipment again and playing the small colleges—they weren't big schools, but they were good teams," he said in a 2017 interview. "I was hurt the first year, but in the second year, I was able to come back in much better shape."

Playing for the Goshawks was definitely a part-time activity. "You had a job there to do and football was secondary," Staubach said. "We practiced about an hour and a half most every day, but that wasn't the primary role. Working for supply on the base was a big job."

Quoted in Jay Cope, "Hall of Fame Quarterback Remembers Goshawks Playing Time," United States Navy, August 28, 2017. www.navy.mil.

---

the Cowboys to ten straight victories, including a dominating 24–3 victory over the Miami Dolphins in Super Bowl VI in 1972. It was the first Super Bowl title for Dallas. That game also marked the moment Staubach became a Cowboys legend. He earned the game's MVP honor, passing for 119 yards and two touchdowns, while rushing for 18 yards. Staubach actually loved to scramble and run when he could, earning him the nickname "Roger Dodger."

QUARTERBACK STATS

Even though he played only ten seasons with the Cowboys, Staubach set more than a dozen of the team's all-time passing records, including most passing yards and most touchdown passes.

Staubach and the Cowboys won a second Super Bowl title in 1977. They defeated the Denver Broncos, led by Staubach's former Dallas rival, quarterback Craig Morton. Around that time, the Cowboys became known as "America's Team" for their nationwide popularity and success throughout the 1970s. Staubach, for his heroics on the field and career in the navy, earned the nickname "Captain America." Staubach's longtime teammate Randy White told *The Athletic* in 2021, "There was always a chance in any game with Roger out there. We always believed that if any game was tight, Roger would get the points we needed to win. And he always did."[15]

Staubach's Legacy

Staubach retired after the 1979 season. In his eight seasons as starting quarterback for Dallas, he amassed some amazing achievements, including the highest passer rating of all time (although that record has since been broken). He was a six-time Pro Bowler and recorded the highest passer rating in four different seasons (1971, 1973, 1978, and 1979). In fact, 1979 was one

Over his eight seasons as starting quarterback for the Dallas Cowboys, Staubach earned the nickname "Captain America" for his heroics on the field.

of his best seasons, but serious health concerns led him to announce that it would be his last.

Staubach suffered twenty concussions in his college and pro career. After the 1979 season, a neurologist told him that one more concussion could have long-term effects on his brain. Unlike so many other football players who experienced numerous concussions, Staubach was fortunate to have escaped serious brain injury and dementia. After football, he devoted his time to his real estate development business and to raising his five children with Marianne.

One of their children, daughter Michelle, was diagnosed with clinical depression when she was young. While her struggle was largely a private matter for many years, in 2021 Staubach began talking about his family's struggle with mental illness, in large part

After retiring from professional football, Staubach volunteered his time for many mental health–related causes. Here he speaks at the Mayor Mike Rawlings of Dallas Rally Against Domestic Violence on March 23, 2013.

to help the general public know that depression and other mood disorders can affect anyone. Staubach talking about mental illness was especially helpful for the current Cowboys quarterback Dak Prescott, who had recently come forward to share his own struggles with depression. "I'll be honest, I'm not crazy about speaking out on things like this," Staubach said in a 2021 interview. "But we have real mental health problems in this country, and it helps when Michelle tells her story and athletes like Dak share their experiences. The dialogue is a positive, no question."[16]

Staubach's NFL career was shorter than some of the other all-time greats because he did not join the league until he was twenty-seven and he retired early. But the way he has conducted himself both on and off the field made him a hero to countless fans, teammates, and even his legendary Cowboys coach Tom Landry. At the quarterback's 1985 Pro Football Hall of Fame induction, Landry introduced Staubach this way:

> You know in any profession, there are two ways to make a winner. How he performs his job and, more importantly, how he performs as a human being. Roger Staubach is an all-pro in both categories. We are here today to honor Roger for his achievements as a professional football player and rightfully so, but if there is a Hall of Fame for people, they better save a spot for him there, too.[17]

Joe Montana: Joe Cool

For many legendary athletes, there is a single play or performance early in their careers that alerts the world that greatness is to follow. Joe Montana's star-making moment happened in the playoffs at the end of just his first full season as starting quarterback for the San Francisco 49ers. Against the Dallas Cowboys in the National Football Conference (NFC) Championship Game on January 10, 1982, the Niners were down 27–21 with less than five minutes left in the game. Starting at San Francisco's eleven-yard line, with almost the entire length of the field ahead of him, Montana completed six passes and moved his team down to Dallas's six-yard line.

With the Cowboys' defense digging in for the final minute of play and the berth in the Super Bowl on the line, the Niners faced third down. Seemingly unfazed by the pressure of the moment, Montana took the snap from center and immediately rolled out to his right. Seeing wide receiver Dwight Clark breaking in the same direction at the back of the end zone, an off-balance Montana sailed the ball into the corner of the end zone to a spot where only Clark could reach it. Clark leaped to pull down the pass for the tying touchdown. The play soon became known simply as "the Catch," and after kicker Ray Wersching kicked the extra point to give San Francisco the lead, the Niners were vaulted into their first Super Bowl appearance. Montana was on his way to one of the greatest and most exciting careers of any NFL quarterback. After the game, San Francisco's quarterbacks coach Sam Wyche said, "Joe does so many intelligent things you can't coach. He has so much poise and savvy. He just has the right stuff."[18]

That comeback in that game was one of thirty-one fourth-quarter comebacks in Montana's remarkable career. As much as any single game, it showed his calm, confident style of play. Montana soon earned the nicknames "Joe Cool" and "the Comeback Kid." Before his career was over, Montana would be a four-time Super Bowl champion and a lock for the Pro Hall of Fame.

The Montanas of Monongahela

Joe Montana was born on June 11, 1956, in New Eagle, a tiny coal-mining town just outside of Pittsburgh in Pennsylvania. He grew up in nearby Monongahela, a town with a population under nine thousand. His father, Joe Montana Sr., managed a finance company. His mother, Theresa, also worked at the finance company. Joe was their only child. He grew up playing baseball, basketball, and football, though basketball was his favorite.

There were countless father-and-son games of catch in the backyard, and Montana's parents seldom missed one of their son's football, basketball, or baseball games. "They taught me to never quit and to strive to be my best," Montana said of his parents during his induction into the Pro Football Hall of Fame in 2000. "They were always there. They took me where I wanted to be, where I needed to be and got me there on time and made tremendous sacrifices to make sure I had things that they never had."[19]

Montana went on to star at Ringgold High School in Monongahela, becoming a national high school All-American his senior year. He received several college scholarship offers, including

> **QUARTERBACK STATS**
>
> Joe Montana was the first player to earn three Super Bowl MVP awards. Tom Brady went on to break that record with five MVP honors. Patrick Mahomes also has three Super Bowl MVP awards.

The Chicken Soup Game

In Joe Montana's final game with Notre Dame, a Cotton Bowl matchup with the University of Houston, the temperature dropped to well below zero. It felt even colder with wind gusting across the stadium. Montana's own temperature dropped, too, as he battled the flu. With a temperature of about 96°F (36°C; more than two degrees lower than normal), Montana was led into the locker room late in the second quarter. The training staff covered him in warm blankets and fed him chicken soup, keeping him inside even after the start of the second half. Out on the field, Houston jumped out to a 34–12 lead. Insisting he felt better and could play, Montana jogged back to the sideline to the cheers of Notre Dame fans early in the third quarter. As was his style, Montana orchestrated an amazing comeback, including three touchdown drives in the game's final eight minutes, to secure a victory in what became known in Notre Dame sports history as "the Chicken Soup Game."

some for basketball. However, he wanted to play football at Notre Dame, in part because his favorite football player—Pittsburgh Steelers quarterback Terry Hanratty—had gone to Notre Dame.

Notre Dame and a National Championship

Montana received a football scholarship to Notre Dame in 1974, but he did not see much action during his first couple of years. At the start of the 1977 season, Montana was still on the bench, playing behind quarterbacks Rusty Lisch and Gary Forystek. In the third game of the season, at home against Purdue, Lisch struggled and Forystek suffered a career-ending injury. Montana came in early in the fourth quarter with Notre Dame down by ten points and calmly led his team to victory. The win assured his place as Notre Dame's starting quarterback.

Notre Dame then won nine games in a row, including a huge 38–10 upset victory over then top-ranked University of Texas in the 1978 Cotton Bowl. This was long before college football had a playoff and a championship game. Back then, whatever team finished first on a poll of college football coaches and sportswriters at the end of the season would be crowned national champion. Notre Dame's 11–1 record and Cotton Bowl performance was enough for the team to win the Associated Press National Championship.

A Dynasty in San Francisco

The 1978 season was Montana's last with the Fighting Irish. Despite his share of comeback victories and late-game heroics at Notre Dame, Montana was not regarded as a top NFL prospect. Scouts questioned his arm strength and other attributes. The San Francisco 49ers finally took Montana in the third round of the 1979 NFL Draft.

When Montana arrived in San Francisco, the Niners were coming off a 2–14 season and a long history of football mediocrity. But San Francisco had a new coach named Bill Walsh, who was perfecting what became known as the West Coast offense. It was actually a philosophy Walsh developed when he was an

Joe Montana prepares to pass the ball at the San Francisco 49ers training camp in Rocklin, California, on August 4, 1988.

QUARTERBACK STATS

Joe Montana holds the San Francisco 49ers' records for passing yards (35,124), passing touchdowns (244), passing attempts (4,600), and completions (2,929).

assistant coach with the Cincinnati Bengals. The offense featured short, perfectly timed and precise passes to pick up six to eight yards per attempt. The idea was that even short passes would gain more yards than most rushing attempts usually pick up. And by putting the ball into the hands of speedy receivers, teams might also see those short gains turn into longer, breakaway gains.

Montana was the backup to Niners' starter Steve DeBerg until halfway through the 1980 season, when DeBerg got hurt. DeBerg was traded to Denver in the offseason, and Montana became the full-time starter in 1981. Directing the West Coast offense in 1982, Montana set an NFL record with five consecutive three-hundred-yard passing games. Through Montana's last season with San Francisco in 1992, he guided the Niners to nine NFC West Division titles and four Super Bowl victories. Montana still holds a couple of Super Bowl records, including most passes without an interception (122).

The Cradle of Quarterbacks

Joe Montana became famous winning four Super Bowls with the San Francisco 49ers. But he grew up on the other side of the country in a region that produced several other all-time great quarterbacks. Montana was born in Monongahela, Pennsylvania, about 25 miles (40 km) south of Pittsburgh. That part of western Pennsylvania also produced Hall of Fame quarterbacks Johnny Unitas, Joe Namath, Jim Kelly, and Dan Marino. Other former NFL quarterbacks from the area include Jeff Hostetler, Terrelle Pryor, Bruce Gradkowski, George Blanda, and many others. In all, more than two dozen NFL quarterbacks grew up within a 50-mile radius (80 km) of Pittsburgh, earning the region the nickname "the Cradle of Quarterbacks." It is not clear why so many quarterbacks have come from the area, though western Pennsylvania does have a long football history, going back to the earliest days of the pro game in the late 1890s. College and NFL games in the area often sell out, and it is not unusual for high school games to draw more than ten thousand fans on an autumn Friday night.

Montana's greatest Super Bowl performance was his last in the big game. In Super Bowl XXIV, following the 1990 season, Montana threw for five touchdown passes and coolly guided his team to a Super Bowl record of fifty-five points. In a *Sports Illustrated* profile of Montana following the 1990 season, NFL writer Paul Zimmerman wrote,

> He put together a remarkable season, the best any quarterback has ever had, according to the NFL's rating system. And he was even better in the playoffs and Super Bowl XXIV, reaching a level of brilliance that had never been seen in postseason football. Which leaves only one question to ask about this remarkable 11-year veteran: Is he the greatest quarterback ever to play the game?[20]

Quarterback Controversy

Even with all of his regular-season and Super Bowl success, Montana spent his last couple of seasons in San Francisco looking over his shoulder at his new backup, Steve Young. Whenever Montana struggled and Young came in and excelled, fans and sportswriters began to wonder whether the Niners should trade Montana to make room for Young in the starting lineup.

Though Montana was privately bothered by the controversy, he never let on publicly. Instead, after the team stumbled at the start of the 1988 season—with Young and Montana splitting playing time—Montana took over the full-time starting duties and led San Francisco to another division title and Super Bowl appearance. And with his team down 16–13 with just over three minutes left in the game, Montana reminded fans, teammates, and coaches why he had long ago earned the nickname "the Comeback Kid." Montana led the offense on a ninety-two-yard touchdown drive to win the game—and the Niners' third Super Bowl championship—with thirty-four seconds left on the clock.

Montana calls a play during Super Bowl XIX on January 21, 1985. The Niners prevailed over the Miami Dolphins in the matchup.

To Canton by Way of Kansas City

To make sure there was no doubt who should be the number one quarterback, Montana powered the Niners to the NFL's best record (14–2) the following season and a fourth Super Bowl win. The 1990 season looked to be more of the same. The team again posted an NFL-best 14–2 record but struggled in the NFC Championship Game and lost. Montana also suffered a serious elbow injury after being sacked by New York Giants defensive lineman Leonard Marshall.

Montana missed the entire 1991 season and part of 1992. At that point, Young was the established starter, and Montana did not want to be his backup. After the 1992 season ended, Montana requested a trade. Figuring the three-time Super Bowl MVP might still have a little more magic left, the Kansas City Chiefs traded for Montana in the spring of 1993.

In the Chiefs' summer training camp, many of Montana's new teammates acted like fans. The team's general manager, Carl Peterson, told ESPN,

On Joe's first day, when the defense was done and it was time to switch to offense, not one defensive player left the practice building. They all sat down around the perimeter to watch because they wanted to see Joe Montana play. That's what those guys thought of the trade. It gave everybody hope we could win a championship. That's why it was such a special time.[21]

Montana played only two seasons with Kansas City, reaching the American Football Conference (AFC) championship after the 1993 season and losing in the first round of the playoffs in 1994. Injuries and time made it clear that Montana was at the end of his career. In the spring of 1995, at age thirty-eight, he announced his retirement.

Montana kept busy in retirement, starting an investment firm with a couple of former teammates and a commercial bank in New York. He also owns a winery and stays busy with a horse farm near San Francisco. He and his wife, Jennifer, have four kids, including two sons who played college football. Montana also works with the Make-A-Wish Foundation, a nonprofit organization that provides children with serious illnesses or disabilities memorable experiences and meetings with superstar athletes and other celebrities.

> **QUARTERBACK STATS**
>
> Joe Montana is one of only two starting quarterbacks to win a national championship in college and a Super Bowl in the NFL. The other is Hall of Famer Joe Namath.

In 2005, Montana was inducted into the Pro Football Hall of Fame in Canton, Ohio. And though many of his records and achievements have been topped since then, Montana is still considered one of the greatest, most clutch quarterbacks in the history of the game. "There have been, and will be, much better arms and legs and much better bodies on quarterbacks in the NFL," Montana's former 49er teammate Randy Cross told ESPN. "But if you have to win a game or score a touchdown or win a championship, the only guy to get is Joe Montana."[22]

John Elway: Bronco for Life

Before John Elway took his first snap as quarterback of the Denver Broncos in 1983, the NFL had seen just a handful of players who were great passers but also could rush for big gains. Called dual-threat quarterbacks, they are much more common in today's game than they were just a decade or two ago. Until recently, most successful professional quarterbacks had been players who dropped back to pass and limited their running to scrambling behind the line of scrimmage as they waited for an open receiver.

Elway was a different kind of quarterback. He became only the second NFL quarterback to throw for more than forty thousand yards and rush for more than three thousand yards in his career. But as Elway passed and rushed his way to five Super Bowl appearances—winning two—football coaches at all levels took notice. Before long, quarterbacks who could make big plays with their arms and their legs started dominating the pro games. Recent quarterback sensations Lamar Jackson, Jalen Hurts, Josh Allen, and Kyler Murray are the descendants of the quarterback position redefined by John Albert Elway Jr.

The Son of a Coach

Elway and his twin sister, Jana, were born in Port Angeles, Washington, in 1960, the younger siblings of an older sister named Lee Ann. Their father, Jack, was then the head football coach at Port Angeles High School. Elway grew up moving with his family every few years as Jack's coaching career took him to places like the University of Montana; Washington State University; and California State University, Northridge. In Southern California, Elway played football at Granada Hills High School, racking up victories, drawing interest from college scouts from all over the country, and impressing his own father, who had seen countless young football players in his coaching career.

After an especially outstanding game one night, Jack and Elway's mother, Jan, walked back to their car. "Jan, I wonder if he's as good as I think he is," Jack said, to which his wife replied that if he did not know, who would. "Well, I think he's the best I've ever seen."[23]

QUARTERBACK STATS

John Elway is the only NFL player to pass for more than three thousand yards and rush for more than two hundred yards in seven straight seasons.

Even before he got to high school, Elway was all about winning and excelling. In youth football games, Elway's competitive nature often got the best of him, and his father frequently had to remind him that it was not okay to yell at his teammates if they made a mistake. Games of football, basketball, or baseball in the backyard became training sessions, as Elway often pleaded with his dad for just a few more minutes of playing, even after the sun had already set. Jack explained Elway's constant desire to improve in a 1998 interview before his son's fourth Super Bowl: "I'd tell him something, then he'd ask questions, then he'd do it. Once you show him how to do something, he has it. He has always had a knack for working on the little things."[24]

During his senior year in high school, Elway received many college offers, including one from his dad, then the head coach at San Jose State. But Elway's father urged his son to attend a university with a bigger and better football program. So, Elway opted for Stanford University—not exactly a football powerhouse, but a top-ranked academic school and one that had produced several NFL quarterbacks. Elway majored in economics and set numerous

33

Stanford and Pacific-10 Conference passing records. His seventy-seven career touchdown passes are still a Stanford record. However, Stanford compiled only a 20–23 record with Elway at quarterback. The team also never made it to a postseason bowl during his time there. Elway, nevertheless, was viewed as a top NFL prospect.

High Expectations in the Mile-High City

Elway was the first player selected in the 1983 NFL Draft. He went to the Baltimore Colts, who then traded him to the Denver Broncos. The pressure to be a superstar came on quick, and expectations only grew as coaches and teammates watched him throw during preseason minicamps. Head coach Dan Reeves said at the time, "He's just got a super arm. You see the velocity, the accuracy and the authority, but what really amazes me is that he puts it where he's aiming it."[25]

It was an up-and-down first season for Elway, though it did include an amazing fourth-quarter comeback against the Colts. Down 19–0 at the start of the fourth quarter, Elway threw three touchdown passes, including the game winner for a 21–19 win.

Elway laughs with his father after the 1983 NFL Draft, where he was picked by the Baltimore Colts. The Colts immediately traded Elway to the Denver Broncos.

The Elway Cross

Beginning in his freshman year at Stanford, John Elway developed the reputation of throwing a football so hard and so fast that his receivers often had a tough time catching it. He reportedly broke fingers on the hands of two Stanford receivers. It got to the point where his receivers had to learn how to trap the ball with their bodies rather than put their fingers in harm's way reaching out for a pass. But the passes would still hit the receivers with such velocity that the ball's point—a cross made up of the football's four seams—often left a mark on a receiver's chest. That mark became known as "the Elway cross."

By the end of his career, Elway had set an NFL record with forty-seven game-tying or game-winning fourth-quarter comebacks.

Though he showed some flashes of greatness during his rookie season, he struggled, too, at one point losing the starting job to veteran Steve DeBerg. But in just his second season, having officially taken the starting job back from DeBerg, Elway led the Broncos to a first-place finish in the AFC West. By 1986, Elway's fourth season in Denver, he really had the Broncos' offense rolling. They scored 378 points that year, sixth best in the NFL, and finished with an 11–5 regular-season record.

The Drive to His First Super Bowl

The legend of John Elway in Denver firmly took root in the playoffs after the 1986 regular season. On the way to his first Super Bowl, Elway orchestrated a thrilling playoff comeback victory over the Cleveland Browns—culminating in what is simply known as "the Drive." With Denver down 20–13 and just over five minutes to play in regulation, the Broncos took control of the ball on their own two-yard line—ninety-eight yards away from the Cleveland end zone and a chance to tie the game. During the next five minutes, through a combination of passes and his own rushing, Elway moved the ball ninety-three yards. The final play led to a touchdown and forced the game into overtime. Denver kicked

QUARTERBACK STATS

John Elway started five Super Bowls, winning two and losing three. The only quarterback with more Super Bowl starts is Tom Brady, with ten starts and a record of 7–3.

a field goal in the extra time to win the AFC Championship and move on to the Super Bowl. "John Elway, unequivocally, is the best clutch player ever to play the game,"[26] recalled former Cleveland wide receiver Brian Brennan, who could only watch from the sidelines that day as Elway picked the Browns' defense apart.

For much of Elway's career in Denver, the Broncos put together exciting, winning regular seasons only to find frustration and defeat in the postseason. "The Drive" wound up being the high point of the season, as the Broncos lost Super Bowl XXI to the New York Giants 39–20. Denver, following another sensational season under Elway's leadership, made it to the Super Bowl the next year. And again, the Broncos lost a lopsided affair—this time 42–10 to the Washington Redskins. Two years later, Denver made it back to the Super Bowl, though Elway's regular-season performance had been inconsistent. The result in Super Bowl XXIV was much the same, as Denver lost to Joe Montana and the San Francisco 49ers by a score of 55–10. It would be a long time before Elway and the Broncos would get another chance to win it all.

John Elway, a New York Yankee?

The 1983 NFL Draft is best remembered as having one of the greatest quarterback classes ever. Six quarterbacks were selected in the first round, with Elway going first to the Baltimore Colts (who moved to Indianapolis the following season). However, Elway had made it clear he did not want to play for the Colts and their coach, Frank Kush. He insisted that he would play baseball for the New York Yankees organization, which had drafted him in 1981 and still held his rights. The Colts, who had the first pick overall, tried to negotiate a trade before the draft but could not make the deal in time. So even knowing Elway's claim that he would play baseball rather than play for the Colts, Baltimore still drafted him first. Denver, with the fourth pick, took offensive lineman Chris Hinton (who Baltimore also wanted) and eventually traded him, a 1984 draft pick, and backup quarterback Mark Herrmann to the Colts for Elway.

John Elway lines up for the pass in an October 19, 1997, matchup against the Oakland Raiders in Oakland, California.

Super Bowl Success . . . Finally

During the 1990s Denver continued to play well and reached the playoffs most years, but there was a growing sense that time was running out for Elway. But in 1997, Elway seemed to recapture some magic, leading Denver to a 12–4 record and a berth in Super Bowl XXXII. Given his struggles in previous Super Bowls, many people wondered whether this would be the year he would finally win it all or if the season would end on another sour note. Fans made it clear they were rooting for Elway as much as the team itself. "I don't know if I like being the sentimental favorite," Elway told reporters prior to the game. "There are a lot of people who might not get another chance to win a Super Bowl, not just me."[27]

In the game, the Broncos were going up against the heavily favored Green Bay Packers and their outstanding quarterback Brett Favre. Denver kept the contest close throughout, but a remarkable run by Elway near the end of the third quarter gave Denver's fans reason to believe that this might finally be their year. With the score tied at 17, and the Broncos facing third down and six yards to go on Green Bay's twelve-yard line, Elway dropped back to pass. Unable to find an open receiver, he tucked the ball and took off running. Approaching the six-yard line and a first down, Elway leaped headfirst against three defenders. They hit him so hard that he spun around 360 degrees in the air and landed facing his own goal line. Elway somehow held on to the ball for a first down and then jumped up and pumped his fist to the Denver sideline. Paul Maguire, who was announcing the game on television, said, "How bad does John Elway want to win this football game?"[28] Though it was not designed that way, the play was later nicknamed "the Helicopter" because of Elway's aerial spin. It is still considered one of the most exciting plays in Super Bowl history and one of Elway's most memorable moments.

QUARTERBACK STATS

John Elway holds the record for most career Super Bowl rushing touchdowns by a quarterback, with four. He rushed for one touchdown in four separate Super Bowl appearances.

The Broncos scored two plays later to take the lead. Green Bay managed to tie the game again, but Elway, inspired by the roars of the crowd, once again led Denver down the field. The Broncos scored a field goal, which gave them their first-ever Super Bowl title.

The next season Denver went to the Super Bowl again, this time defeating the Atlanta Falcons 34–19. A few months after this second Super Bowl win, Elway announced his retirement at the age of thirty-eight. That fall, the Broncos retired his number 7 jersey. Five years later, Elway was inducted into the Pro Football Hall of Fame.

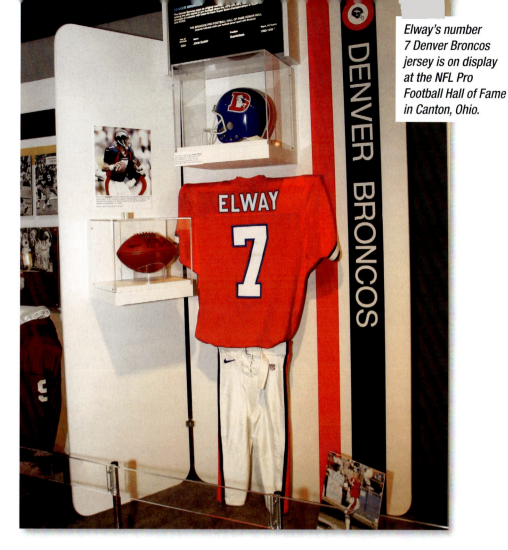

Elway's number 7 Denver Broncos jersey is on display at the NFL Pro Football Hall of Fame in Canton, Ohio.

The Broncos wanted to keep Elway around after his playing days, even if he could not add to his victory totals anymore. The team hired him in 2011 as executive vice president of football operations. The following year, he helped bring Peyton Manning to Denver, where Manning led the team to a Super Bowl title in 2014. In 2023, Elway finally left the Broncos, though he said he would always be available to offer advice or help. Elway has said he hoped to spend more time with his growing family. He and his wife, Janet, have four children and seven grandchildren. When he announced he was leaving the Broncos, Elway said, "I've enjoyed the relationship with the Broncos for a long, long time."[29] Certainly many Broncos fans would say they enjoyed the Elway era in Denver too.

Tom Brady: The GOAT

Nine college quarterbacks were selected in the 2000 NFL Draft. Tom Brady, today considered by many fans and football experts to be the greatest of all time (GOAT), was one of them. But on that day, Brady was just another fairly unremarkable college player hoping to make the NFL. He was drafted in the sixth round (out of seven) by the New England Patriots. The Patriots already had a solid starter in Drew Bledsoe, and Brady had struggled just to get playing time at the University of Michigan. Draft experts, including ESPN's Mel Kiper Jr., liked his consistency and intelligence but were not overwhelmed by his athletic gifts. Kiper projected Brady as a fifth-round pick at best—and not someone who would go on to win seven Super Bowls and dominate the game for twenty-three seasons.

Even Brady would not have predicted anything close to the career he had. In the days leading up to his tenth AFC Championship Game in 2016, Brady admitted in a radio interview that he could not have dreamed he would be on top of the game for so long. He reached his first AFC title game in just his second year in the league. He said, "Fifteen years later, to be a part of 10 of those, I never imagined that any of this was ever even possible. I just knew that I loved the game and I played with so many great teammates who have sacrificed so much."[30]

Montana to Michigan

Brady has loved football for about as long as he can remember. Born in San Mateo, California, in 1977, he grew up rooting for the nearby San Francisco 49ers and idolizing their superstar quarterback Joe Montana. "To have a chance to go to 49ers games on the weekends with him [Brady's dad], my mom . . . throw the ball in the parking lot at the games, those are memories that I'll have forever,"[31] he said in a YouTube video prior to Super Bowl LI, a game that saw the Patriots defeat the Atlanta Falcons 34–28.

Brady's father, Tom Brady Sr., was in the insurance business, and his mother, Galynn, had been a flight attendant before they married and started raising a family. There were four kids in all—Brady and three sisters. Brady grew up playing football, basketball, and baseball, starring in all three sports at Junipero Serra High School in San Mateo. Brady was a power-hitting catcher on the baseball team and was drafted by the Montreal Expos (now the Washington Nationals) when he was a senior.

> **QUARTERBACK STATS**
>
> Tom Brady holds the career record for wins by a quarterback, with 251. The next closest on the career victories list are Brett Favre and Peyton Manning, with 186 wins each.

He became the school's starting quarterback during his junior year and made tapes of his game highlights and sent them to colleges he was interested in attending. The final list of schools included the University of California, Berkeley; the University of California, Los Angeles; the University of Southern California; the University of Illinois; and the University of Michigan. Even though his parents had hoped Brady would go to school in California, he opted for Michigan.

It took some time for Brady to establish himself as the Wolverines' starting quarterback. In 1995, during Brady's first year at Michigan, he was seventh on the depth chart, meaning there were six other quarterbacks ahead of him vying for playing time. He redshirted, meaning he could practice with the team but not play in any games. As a result, he would still have four years of

Tom Brady, then quarterback for the Michigan Wolverines, throws a pass during an NCAA football game against the Penn State Nittany Lions on November 13, 1999, in University Park, Pennsylvania.

eligibility to play after the redshirt season. Brady saw limited action the rest of the 1996 and 1997 seasons. Throughout the 1998 and 1999 seasons, Brady was still competing for a starting job—this time with Drew Henson. Brady eventually earned the full-time quarterback job, ending his college career with a thrilling last-minute win over rival Ohio State and an even more dramatic overtime victory over Alabama in the 2000 Orange Bowl.

The Franchise Changer

Despite his success at Michigan, Brady was not viewed as a top NFL prospect. He did not have the flashy statistics that some other college quarterbacks had. Marshall University's Chad Pennington, for example, threw 115 touchdown passes in college and was the first quarterback drafted in 2000. Brady threw 30 touchdown passes and was the seventh quarterback drafted.

So, when the Patriots took a chance on Brady in the sixth round, no one had especially high expectations. But New England had a new coach in Bill Belichick, who had previously been an assistant coach or head coach with several teams before starting the most successful run of any NFL coach in history. The 2000 season was a letdown, with rookie Tom Brady seeing little action. But in 2001, everything changed.

In the second game of the 2001 season, Bledsoe took a nasty hit while running toward the sideline and suffered internal bleeding. Brady came off the bench, but the Patriots still lost the game. With Brady starting the third game, the Patriots smashed the Colts 44–13. Brady and the Patriots were off and running. They rolled through the rest of the regular season, survived a thriller against the Raiders in the playoffs, and squared up against the heavily favored St. Louis Rams in Super Bowl XXXVI in 2002.

QUARTERBACK STATS

Tom Brady won seven Super Bowls. That is more than any franchise has won. New England and Pittsburgh each have six Super Bowl victories in their history, and the 49ers and Cowboys each have five.

The Brady-Manning Rivalry

Tom Brady joined the Patriots in 2000, two years after the Indianapolis Colts drafted Peyton Manning. It did not have the makings of an all-time great rivalry at the time, but soon football fans would be treated to one of the most amazing duels in NFL history. Over the next fifteen years, Brady and Manning would win seven league MVPs and six Super Bowls between them, while also setting and breaking numerous records. In 2007, Brady set a single-season record with fifty touchdown passes. In 2013, Manning broke the record, tossing fifty-five touchdowns. They played each other seventeen times in their careers, with the Patriots winning eleven of those matchups. And though Brady often seemed to have the upper hand, he was always quick to praise his AFC rival, telling ESPN in 2021, "I always looked up to Peyton because he was a little older than me and was always doing things the right way. His team was always in it. I know our teams had a rivalry against one another, but when you went against a Peyton-led team, you were going against the best team in the league."

Quoted in Mike Reiss, "Tom Brady to Join Peyton Manning's Section for Hall of Fame Induction Ceremony," ESPN, August 5, 2021. www.espn.com.

> **QUARTERBACK STATS**
>
> Tom Brady is the only player in NFL history to have beaten every other team in the league at least once. (He was finally able to beat New England after he signed with Tampa Bay.)

New England was up 17–3 late in the game, but St. Louis fought back to tie the game with a minute and a half left in regulation play. The Patriots had no time-outs, but instead of just running out the clock to take their chances in overtime, Brady completed five pinpoint passes and guided the Patriots from their own seventeen-yard line down to the Rams' thirty-one-yard line, where he spiked the ball to stop the clock with seven seconds left. Television announcer (and former Oakland Raiders coach) John Madden said, "I'll tell you, what Tom Brady just did, gives me goosebumps."[32] New England kicker Adam Vinatieri then kicked the winning field goal as time expired, giving New England and Brady their first of many more Super Bowl victories.

Over the next seventeen years, under the leadership of Brady and Belichick, New England returned to the Super Bowl eight more times, winning five more championships. Brady earned four Super Bowl MVP awards; three regular-season MVP awards; and countless other awards, honors, and NFL records.

Brady lifts the Vince Lombardi Trophy as Patriots head coach Bill Belichick looks on after defeating the Atlanta Falcons in Super Bowl LI at NRG Stadium in Houston, Texas, on February 5, 2017.

Is Tom Brady the GOAT?

Sports fans love ranking teams and players and debating who is the greatest of all time in a particular sport. Basketball fans seem to never stop debating the LeBron James–Michael Jordan GOAT question. As for Tom Brady, the seven Super Bowl wins, the longevity, and the all-time passing records make a pretty good case that he deserves that title. NFL greats such as Jerry Rice, Emmitt Smith, Ray Lewis, Brett Favre, Troy Aikman, and Randy Moss have, at various times, labeled Brady as the GOAT.

But what does Brady think? In many interviews through the years, he has repeatedly pushed back on the compliment, saying it makes him feel uncomfortable. In 2018, after winning his record fifth Super Bowl, Brady said, "I don't see myself in that way. That's not a value that I put on me playing. I play for the enjoyment of the game. I play for the camaraderie with my teammates, and I play to win." He may not like to hear it, but plenty of his peers and sports fans will be calling him the GOAT for a long time.

Quoted in Michael Hurley, "Tom Brady Just Casually Dropped the Cockiest Line of His Whole Career," CBS Sports, July 21, 2021. www.cbsnews.com.

The Records

When Tom Brady retired from the NFL in 2023, he owned more than thirty career NFL records. Among them are passing yards (89,214), passing touchdowns (649), and completions (7,753). And those are just his regular-season numbers. As for the playoffs and Super Bowls, Brady holds a similar collection of records. They include most career postseason passing yards (13,400), postseason passing touchdowns (88), and postseason wins by a starting quarterback (35). His Super Bowl achievements include most appearances (10), MVPs (5), touchdown passes (21), and game-winning drives (6).

Perhaps Brady's most remarkable Super Bowl performance was in Super Bowl LI in 2017, in which New England found itself down 28–3 in the third quarter. Just when it seemed like the Atlanta Falcons were going to show Brady and company their worst Super Bowl defeat, Brady once again performed magic on the field. He orchestrated the greatest comeback in Super Bowl history, leading the Patriots to twenty-five unanswered points to force overtime. The Patriots won 34–28 in the first overtime in the Super Bowl, and Brady set Super Bowl records with sixty-two passing attempts and 466 passing yards.

And along with all the numbers, Brady also earned the respect of his peers. The list of other NFL greats who have called him the best ever include Hall of Famers Jerry Rice (maybe the best receiver of all time), running back Barry Sanders, linebacker Ray Lewis, quarterback Aaron Rodgers, and so on. Hall of Fame tight end Shannon Sharpe once said, "Tom Brady is the greatest football player in the 97-year history of the NFL."[33]

Brady the Buccaneer

Brady's storied career with the New England Patriots came to an end twenty years after it began. In the spring of 2020, Brady announced he would not sign a new contract with the team. Immediately, the football world started speculating about where Brady might go next or if he might actually retire altogether. Nobody had to wait long. Three days after Brady said goodbye to New England, he said hello to Tampa, signing a two-year contract with the Tampa Bay Buccaneers.

Brady's arrival instantly made Tampa Bay a contender. Brady's number 12 Bucs jersey quickly became a bestseller. But the 2020 season, like so many things that year, was drastically affected by the COVID-19 pandemic. Some teams played games with no one in attendance; other franchises allowed limited fan attendance,

This Brady #144 autographed rookie card sold for $3.1 million at a 2021 auction, making it the world's most valuable football card at the time.

46

but spectators were spread out to reduce the odds of infection. Through that unusual season, Brady and the Bucs dominated and eventually reached the Super Bowl, where they defeated the defending champion Kansas City Chiefs.

Retirement(s)

A year after he helped Tampa Bay win its second Super Bowl and his first not as a New England Patriot, Tom Brady hinted that he might finally be ready to retire. His play in 2021 was average at best, and rumors began circulating that one of the all-time great sporting careers was about to end. Word had gotten out that Brady had been struggling with a knee injury for most of 2020 and part of 2021. The sports media world speculated for months about Brady's future.

Brady announced his retirement on February 1, 2022, only to change his mind forty days later and return for the 2022 season. Though he had flashes of his former brilliance, Brady was unable to will his team back to the Super Bowl stage, where he had shone so brightly so many times before. So, on February 1, 2023, exactly one year after his first retirement announcement, Brady declared he was officially retiring with no plans for another comeback.

Brady, however, only retired from playing football. He opted to stick close to the game, signing a lucrative deal with Fox Sports to join its commentator lineup in the 2024 NFL season. Ready for a new challenge, Brady said, "It's something that's new, it's outside of my comfort zone. And I'm excited to get out there and try something and see how I do. But it's got to be about what my preparation is and what my work ethic is. And hopefully a lot of the things that I've done in my career have prepared me for that."[34]

Patrick Mahomes: The King of Kansas City

It can be difficult to evaluate someone's career before it is over, but in Patrick Mahomes's first seven seasons he has smashed records. And he has accomplished more than most quarterbacks could dream of for an entire career. He has played in four Super Bowls and is one of only five quarterbacks ever to win three. Since becoming the starter in 2018, Mahomes has led the Kansas City Chiefs to a remarkable six straight AFC Championship Games. AFC titles in 2022 and 2023 were both followed by Super Bowl wins.

What makes Mahomes's early career and accomplishments so remarkable is the way he performs. He improvises. He takes brutal hits and jumps right up for the next play. He runs for long gains. He seldom loses his cool. He makes every type of throw: firing perfect spirals in between defenders to a receiver far downfield, sidearm passes, underhand tosses, and basketball-style jump shots.

Mahomes's teammate and favorite target, tight end Travis Kelce, says it is time to give Mahomes the title of best ever. "He's doing things that very few quarterbacks have done," Kelce said after the Chiefs' 2024 Super Bowl victory over the San Francisco 49ers. "Give that man his crown!"[35]

Football or Baseball?

Mahomes was born in Tyler, Texas, in 1995 and grew up in nearby Whitehouse, Texas. He is the oldest of four children. His father, Pat Mahomes, was a Major League Baseball pitcher. His mother, Randi Martin, has an event-planning business. Mahomes spent many of his early years running around on baseball fields with his dad, learning the ins and outs of that sport. He also played basketball. Football did not enter into his life until middle school, when he began playing on defense as a safety. Once he reached high school, Mahomes switched to quarterback, but he still did not become the starter until early in his junior year. Though he improved quickly, he did so without attending high-profile quarterback camps that so many elite high school quarterbacks attend every summer. Mahomes never had a private quarterback coach, as many of his peers around the nation did. "There's no guru; there's no camps," his college coach, Kliff Kingsbury, said. "He's just a natural thrower."[36] Mahomes has said he thinks baseball pitching and playing basketball made him a better quarterback.

Pat Mahomes actually tried to talk his son out of a football career while Mahomes was still in high school. His dad told him that baseball seemed like his best sport, so why was he wasting all this time playing football? On a 2021 podcast, Pat Mahomes said of that conversation with

QUARTERBACK STATS

Patrick Mahomes has won three Super Bowls and has been the MVP in all three games.

his son, "He looked at me and said, 'Dad, you know, I just want to play with my friends. I can't see myself on Friday nights being up in the stands and watching them play and not being a part of it.' So that was kinda it for the conversation."[37]

A Legend in Lubbock

Kingsbury recruited Mahomes to Texas Tech University in Lubbock. Bigger football schools such as the University of Alabama and University of Texas had expressed some interest in Mahomes.

Named the Texas Associated Press Sports Editors football player of the year for 2013, a high school–age Patrick Mahomes holds his award as he poses with his father, Pat; younger brother, Jackson; and mother, Randi, on December 20, 2013, in Whitehouse, Texas.

But they were either lukewarm about his chances to get real playing time or wanted him to change positions.

Determined to play quarterback in a major college program, Mahomes arrived at Texas Tech and quickly established himself as one of the school's all-time greats. Even though he skipped his senior year to enter the NFL Draft, Mahomes put up numbers that place him among the school's top passers of all time. He ranks third in Texas Tech history with 11,252 passing yards, just behind Mahomes's college coach, Kingsbury, who was the Red Raiders' quarterback from 1998 to 2002. Mahomes is also third among Texas Tech quarterbacks with ninety-three career touchdown passes, and he ranks second with twenty-two rushing touchdowns. Mahomes also holds the Red Raiders' record for most passing yards in a single game with 734 against Oklahoma in 2016.

At Texas Tech, Mahomes developed a reputation for improvising when a planned play did not work or when the defense surprised him with a blitz or other unexpected scheme. Some critics said Mahomes was undisciplined, scrambling around the field making wild throws or breaking off a big run in a situation that called for a pass. But his teammates and coaches loved it. "He's pretty special," said his former offensive coordinator, Eric Morris. "It's fun to watch him create these plays and find people downfield. How accurate he throws the ball on the run is what's really remarkable to me."[38]

Taking Over in Kansas City

Leading up to the 2017 NFL Draft, three quarterbacks emerged as that year's best options: Mahomes, Mitch Trubisky from the University of North Carolina, and DeShaun Watson from Clemson.

Kansas City's head coach, Andy Reid, had his sights set on Mahomes. Reid liked his ability to improvise and make throws from all angles and from all over the field. Mahomes, Reid felt,

What Mahomes Means to Kansas City

Patrick Mahomes is the undisputed star of the Kansas City Chiefs football team. But he has brought much more to the area than gridiron greatness. Nate Taylor, who covers the Chiefs for *The Athletic*, says that Mahomes has boosted Kansas City in many ways. In 2024 Taylor told CNN,

> He has become an international star, but he's also elevated Kansas City alongside him. The city itself has grown quite a bit. There is more economic impact downtown. The team has been able to convince the NFL—largely because of their success, which is obviously dependent on Mahomes—to have the NFL draft here this past April. Kansas City has a new international airport, it's very nice. All of these things happened after the Chiefs became prominent because they made the best decision in their franchise history.

Mahomes has also invested in the region, becoming a minority owner of the Kansas City Royals baseball team. He and his wife, Brittany, are also co-owners of the Kansas City Current, a member of the National Women's Soccer League.

Quoted in Sam Joseph, "After Winning His Third Super Bowl at Only 28 Years Old, Is It Time to Call Patrick Mahomes the Greatest QB Ever?," CNN, February 12, 2024. www.cnn.com.

QUARTERBACK STATS

Patrick Mahomes has the highest career playoff passer rating at 105.8, only slightly better than his regular-season career passer rating of 103.6, which is second highest behind Aaron Rodgers.

would fit in with the offense he was trying to build in Kansas City. Concerned that Mahomes would be drafted before the Chiefs' pick, Kansas City reached out to several teams, offering additional draft choices for the chance to move up and take Mahomes.

Kansas City traded three draft picks with Buffalo just to get the Bills' tenth pick in the 2017 draft. It was a lot to give up for an untested quarterback, but the move paid off in a hurry. During his first NFL season, Mahomes played backup to Chiefs starter Alex Smith, who led the team to a playoff berth. Coach Reid decided to rest Smith for the team's final regular-season game, giving Mahomes his first start. The rookie played well, and the Chiefs won the game, though they lost the following week in the first round of the playoffs with Smith back as the starter.

Even though Smith was still considered to be a solid NFL quarterback, the Chiefs were ready to put Mahomes at the center of their offense. Kansas City traded Smith to Washington, and Mahomes was named the starter for the upcoming 2018 season. Mahomes's first year as a starter was filled with highs and lows,

The Kansas City Chiefs select Patrick Mahomes of Texas Tech with the tenth pick at the 2017 NFL Draft on April 27, 2017, in Philadelphia, Pennsylvania.

Mahomes's Fast Start

Patrick Mahomes's three Super Bowl victories before the age of thirty is quite an achievement, but his early success has earned him quite a few places in the record books. For example, Mahomes owns the record for most touchdown passes (181), passing yards (22,799), and wins (59) by any quarterback in his first seventy-five games. He was also the fastest quarterback to reach fifteen thousand career passing yards, but then became the fastest to reach twenty thousand career passing yards—doing so in just sixty-seven games. The previous record was held by Matthew Stafford, who reached that goal in seventy-one games. Mahomes also set a record for most touchdown passes in a quarterback's first ten NFL games, with twenty-nine.

including a wild 54–51 loss to the Los Angeles Rams, in which Mahomes threw for 478 yards—the most by any quarterback in a single game that season. Mahomes also led the team to the playoffs. However, Kansas City's promising season came to a sudden end before a home crowd with a 37–31 overtime loss to the New England Patriots in January 2019. Despite Mahomes's three touchdown passes, the Patriots won the AFC Championship.

Mahomes Reaches the Top

After the disappointing and frustrating end to the 2018 season, Mahomes vowed to not only get back to the AFC Championship Game but also to the Super Bowl. He once again played brilliantly throughout the year, again reaching the 2019 AFC title game, this time against the Tennessee Titans. Down 17–7 in the second quarter, Mahomes sparked a remarkable comeback in which he threw three touchdown passes and ran for a twenty-seven-yard touchdown. The Chiefs held on for a 35–24 win and a spot in the team's first Super Bowl since 1970.

Super Bowl LIV, played in 2020, pitted the Chiefs against the 49ers. Down by ten points late in the third quarter, Kansas City rallied in the fourth. The Chiefs scored twenty-one unanswered points behind Mahomes's 286 yards passing and two touchdown throws, as well as his 29 yards rushing and one touchdown run. Kansas City prevailed with a 31–20 victory.

QUARTERBACK STATS

At age twenty-six, Patrick Mahomes became the youngest player to win league MVP and Super Bowl MVP in the same season.

The next two seasons ended in frustration for Mahomes and the Chiefs. In 2021, the Tampa Bay Buccaneers and their new quarterback, Tom Brady, stung the Chiefs 31–9 in Super Bowl LV. And in 2022, the Chiefs lost in overtime to the Cincinnati Bengals in the AFC Championship Game. The Bengals went on to lose to the Los Angeles Rams in Super Bowl LVI.

But in 2023 and 2024, the Chiefs won back-to-back Super Bowls, and Mahomes earned MVP honors in both of those games, due in large part to the late-game magic he conjured up each time.

In 2023, with five minutes to play in Super Bowl LVII, the Philadelphia Eagles tied the Chiefs and looked to have all the momentum. But Mahomes then drove the ball almost the length of the field, using up all but eight seconds, which Chiefs kicker Harrison Butker used to kick the winning field goal. And in Super Bowl LVIII in 2024, the game was tied at the end of regulation. In overtime, the Niners kicked a field goal, but the Chiefs responded with a lengthy drive down the field, culminating in a three-yard touchdown pass from Mahomes to wide receiver Mecole Hardman.

A Legacy of Winning and Giving

Mahomes's Super Bowl titles and jaw-dropping plays have sparked countless conversations about whether he is on his way to supplanting Tom Brady as the NFL's greatest quarterback of all time. But Mahomes is not ready to have the GOAT conversation just yet. "We're not done, we've got a young team, we're gonna keep this thing going,"[39] Mahomes said after Super Bowl LVIII in 2024. But Chiefs beat writer Nate Taylor of *The Athletic* said Mahomes has already ascended to a level that few athletes ever reach. Taylor told CNN after Mahomes's third Super Bowl title, "He has now reached a level that is very parallel to Tom Brady or to Joe Montana where, even though it's the ultimate team sport in America, he can redefine what it means to have that one player who can change the outcome between winning and losing."[40]

Mahomes looks to pass under pressure in the third quarter of an NFL game between the Baltimore Ravens and the Kansas City Chiefs on September 5, 2024, in Kansas City, Missouri.

Mahomes has other priorities beyond winning more Super Bowls. He married his high school sweetheart, Brittany, in 2022. They have two children (and in July 2024 announced that they were expecting again). The couple also established a nonprofit group to help children in the Kansas City area called the "15 and the Mahomies Foundation" (*15* is Mahomes's jersey number). The foundation sponsors programs that encourage reading, fitness, and other classroom and health-related projects. Mahomes's foundation also helps match teens with volunteer opportunities in their communities, and each year it gives money to youth-related charities throughout Kansas City—usually fifteen thousand dollars to fifteen different charities. Mahomes, who personally shows up for many of his foundation's events, has also donated time and money to programs like the Boys and Girls Club in Lubbock, Texas. The people who know Mahomes are not surprised that he is so willing to give back. In 2023, Mahomes's former Chiefs teammate Anthony Sherman told KSHB-TV in Kansas City, "As good as he was on the football field, he's a better person."[41]

Introduction:
Passing into History

1. Quoted in Jeff Legwold, "The 2013 Broncos Scored an NFL-record 606 Points . . . and Have Been Forgotten," ESPN, September 27, 2023. www.espn.com.
2. Quoted in NFL.com, "Being a QB Isn't Easy, but the Very Best Share Some Common Traits," August 28, 2009. www.nfl.com.
3. Quoted in Pro Football Hall of Fame, "Gold Jacket Spotlight: Terry Bradshaw's Singular Focus." www.profootballhof.com.
4. Quoted in Nick Kostos, "The Greatest Quarterback of All Time: How Do We Objectively Assess Greatness?," Bleacher Report, March 27, 2013. www.bleacherreport.com.

Chapter One:
Johnny Unitas: The Golden Arm

5. Frank Deford, "The Best There Ever Was," *Sports Illustrated*, September 23, 2002. www.vault.si.com.
6. Quoted in Chris Willis, "Johnny Unitas Week: Monthly Magazines & Annuals*," Pro Football Journal* (blog), May 3, 2016. www.nflfootballjournal.blogspot.com.
7. Quoted in Bob Carter, "Unitas Surprised Them All," ESPN. www.espn.com.
8. Quoted in David Ginsburg, "Hall of Fame QB Unitas Dies at 69," *Lawrence Journal-World*, September 12, 2002. www2.ljworld.com.
9. Quoted in William Nack, "The Wrecking Yard," *Sports Illustrated,* May 7, 2001. www.vault.si.com.
10. Quoted in ESPN Classic, "ESPN Classic Remembers Johnny Unitas," November 19, 2003. www.espn.com.

Chapter Two:
Roger Staubach: Captain America

11. Quoted in Horatio Alger Association, "Roger T. Staubach," 2007. https://horatioalger.org.
12. Quoted in Chris Low, "Staubach's Heisman, Piece by Piece," ESPN, August 15, 2013. www.espn.com.
13. Quoted in Ray Mahon, "Staubach Misses Football, Feels He'd Click as a Pro," *Stars & Stripes*, October 16, 1966. www.stripes.com.

14. Quoted in Bill Livingston, "'Old Rookie' Roger Staubach Provides a Role Model for Cleveland Browns' Brandon Weeden," Cleveland .com, June 15, 2012. www.cleveland.com.
15. Quoted in Jon Machota, "NFL 100: No. 78, Why Roger Staubach Was the 'Greatest Sports Hero of His Time,'" *The Athletic,* July 19, 2021. www.nytimes.com.
16. Quoted in Richie Whitt, "Exclusive: Cowboys Legend Roger Staubach Details Family's Mental-Health Challenges," *Sports Illustrated,* January 20, 2021. www.si.com.
17. Quoted in Pro Football Hall of Fame, "Roger Staubach Hall of Fame Enshrinement Speech." www.profootballhof.com.

Chapter Three:
Joe Montana: Joe Cool
18. Quoted in Joe Gergen, "TSN Archives: 'The Catch' Dooms Dallas, Lifts 49ers in 1981 NFC Championship," *Sporting News*, January 10, 2023. www.sportingnews.com.
19. Quoted in Matt Barrows, "Joe Montana Sr., Father of Famed 49ers Quarterback Dies at Age of 85," *Sacramento Bee,* May 25, 2017. www.sacbee.com.
20. Paul Zimmerman, "Born to Be a Quarterback," *Sports Illustrated,* August 6, 1990. www.vault.si.com.
21. Quoted in Adam Teicher, "Three Things You Might Not Know About Joe Montana Trade," ESPN, April 20, 2018. www.espn.com.
22. Quoted in Larry Schwartz, "Montana Was Comeback King," ESPN. www.espn.com.

Chapter Four:
John Elway: Bronco for Life
23. Quoted in Douglas Looney, "Elway on Elway: A Father's Perspective," *Christian Science Monitor,* January 22, 1988. www.csmonitor .com.
24. Quoted in Looney, "Elway on Elway."
25. Quoted in Jim Saccomano, "Sacco Sez: John Elway's Memorable First Minicamp," Denver Broncos, May 23, 2021. www.denver broncos.com.
26. Quoted in CBS News, "John Elway & 'the Drive,'" May 2, 1999. www.cbs.com.
27. Quoted in Pro Football Hall of Fame, "John Elway, Class of 2004." www.profootballhof.com.
28. Quoted in Vic Vela, "Feeling Down About the Broncos? Remember the Good Old Days—It's the 25th Anniversary of Their First Super Bowl Win," CPR News, January 25, 2023. www.cpr.org.

29. Quoted in Grant Gordon, "John Elway No Longer with Broncos After Consultant Contract Expires," NFL.com, April 4, 2013. www.nfl.com.

Chapter Five:
Tom Brady: The GOAT

30. Quoted in Mike Cole, "Tom Brady's Success Has Surprised Even Tom Brady: 'Beyond What I'd Ever Imagined,'" New England Sports Network, January 18, 2016. www.nesn.com.
31. Quoted in Andrew Pistone, "From the Backyard to the Super Bowl: Looking Back at Tom Brady's and Patrick Mahomes's Childhood," GMTM. www.gmtm.com.
32. Quoted in Nick Gross, "Madden's Call of Super Bowl XXXVI Between Patriots, Rams Was Legendary," NBC Sports Boston, December 29, 2021. www.nbcsportsboston.com.
33. Quoted in Deyscha Smith, "12 NFL Players on What Makes Tom Brady the GOAT," Boston.com, August 17, 2019. www.boston.com.
34. Quoted in Mike Florio, "Tom Brady Closes In on the Start of His Broadcasting Job at Fox," NBC Sports, January 2, 2024. www.nbcsports.com.

Chapter Six:
Patrick Mahomes: The King of Kansas City

35. Quoted in Sam Joseph, "After Winning His Third Super Bowl at Only 28 Years Old, Is It Time to Call Patrick Mahomes the Greatest QB Ever?," CNN, February 12, 2024. www.cnn.com.
36. Quoted in Andy Wittry, "Patrick Mahomes: College Football Career, Stats, Highlights, Records," NCAA, February 11, 2024. www.espn.com.
37. Quoted in John Healy, "Patrick Mahomes' Father Says He Tried Talking Son Out of Football in High School," Audacy, June 23, 2021. www.audacy.com.
38. Quoted in Wittry, "Patrick Mahomes."
39. Quoted in Joseph, "After Winning His Third Super Bowl at Only 28 Years Old, Is It Time to Call Patrick Mahomes the Greatest QB Ever?"
40. Quoted in Joseph, "After Winning His Third Super Bowl at Only 28 Years Old, Is It Time to Call Patrick Mahomes the Greatest QB Ever?"
41. Quoted in Megan Abundis, "Going 360: The Value of Patrick Mahomes to Kansas City," KSHB-TV, February 9, 2023. www.kshb.com.

Books

John Feinstein, *Quarterback: Inside the Most Important Position in Professional Sports.* New York: Anchor, 2019.

George Johnson, *NFL Heroes: The 100 Greatest Players of All Time.* Richmond Hill, Ontario: 2022.

Patrick Mahomes, *Patrick Mahomes: The Rise of a Champion.* Battle Ground, WA: Pediment, 2020.

David Stabler, *Tom Brady vs. Joe Montana: Who Would Win?* Minneapolis: Lerner, 2023.

Internet Sources

Jason Fitz, Jori Epstein, and Charles Robinson, "How Has Drafting the QB Position Changed in the NFL?," Yahoo! Sports, April 18, 2024. www.sports.yahoo.com.

Lyle Graversen, "How Does Patrick Mahomes Compare to Hall of Fame QBs So Far?," Arrowhead Addict, June 26, 2024. www.arrowheadaddict.com.

Elliot Harrison, "Top 25 Quarterbacks of All Time: Patriots' Tom Brady Leads List," NFL.com, July 2, 2019. www.nfl.com.

David Hunt, "Tom Brady: Career Retrospective," Yardbarker, August 25, 2024. www.yardbarker.com.

Dakota Randall, "The Best QBs of All Time," Pro Football Network, May 23, 2024. www.profootballnetwork.com.

Sports Illustrated, "Football's Greatest: Ranking the Top 10 Quarterbacks in NFL History," October 27, 2017. www.si.com.

Robert Zeglinski, "Ranking the 10 Greatest NFL Quarterbacks of All Time," *USA Today,* July 20, 2024. https://ftw.usatoday.com.

Websites

College Football Hall of Fame

www.cfbhall.com

The College Football Hall of Fame, which recognizes the all-time great players in college history, is in Atlanta, Georgia. But there is plenty of college football history and news on this site. Many all-time great pro players are also inducted into the College Football Hall of Fame, which also includes the stories of many athletes whose greatest success was at the college level.

ESPN Football
www.espn.com/nfl
ESPN covers the latest news in the NFL, previews upcoming games, provides highlights from all the games, and lets visitors track how their favorite players are doing week after week. Visitors can keep track of the standings, read columns by some of ESPN's top football writers, and get ongoing draft coverage to get an idea of who the next top NFL quarterback might be.

National Football League (NFL)
www.nfl.com
The NFL includes thirty-two teams, and its main site tracks pro football news for every team as well as schedules, statistics, and history of the game. The website includes player stats and info on contract negotiations, trades, free agent signings, and highlights from around the league.

Pro Football Hall of Fame
www.profootballhof.com
The Pro Football Hall of Fame, located in Canton, Ohio, is filled with items from the game's history, including uniforms and helmets worn by superstars, photographs and videos documenting the game's history, and more. The website provides all kinds of information about the history of the NFL and its greatest players.

Pro Football Reference
www.pro-football-reference.com
This website includes information and statistics about everyone who has played in the NFL, and lists the top players in dozens of categories, from career passing yards to most interceptions. There are also lists of record holders for each team and season-by-season records and information for the NFL or for individual teams and players.

INDEX

Note: Boldface page numbers indicate illustrations.

Allen, Josh, 32
American Football Conference (AFC)
    Championship Games
    Brady, 40
    Elway, 35–36
    Mahomes, 48, 53, 54
    Montana, 31
American Football League (AFL), 10–11
    See also Super Bowls
"America's Team." *See* Dallas Cowboys
Associated Press National
    Championship, 27
Athletic, The, 21, 51, 54
Atlanta Falcons, 38, 45–46

Baltimore Colts
    Elway with, 34, **34**, 36
    Unitas with, 8–13
Baltimore Ravens, 4, 11
basketball's GOAT, 45
Belichick, Bill, 43, 44, **44**
Berry, Raymond, 12
Blanda, George, 28
Bleacher Report, 7
Bledsoe, Drew, 40, 43
Bloomfield Rams, 9
Bradshaw, Terry, 5
Brady, Tom
    AFC Championship Games, 40
    #144 autographed rookie card, **46**
    basic facts about, 41
    as college football player, 40
    as the GOAT, 40, 45
    as high school football player, 41
    injuries, 47
    Manning and, 43
    with Michigan Wolverines, 41–42, **42**
    Montana and, 41
    as MVP, 43, 44, 45
    with New England Patriots, 40, 43–44,
      44
    records set by, 41, 44, 45
    retirement of, 45, 47
    as sports commentator, 47
    Super Bowls, 36, 40, 41, 43–44, **44**,
      45–46, 47, 54
    with Tampa Bay Buccaneers, 46–47,
      54

Brees, Drew, 5, 10, 13
Brennan, Brian, 36
Butker, Harrison, 54

"Catch, the," 24
Chicken Soup Game, the, 26
Cincinnati Bengals, 54
Clark, Dwight, 24
Cleveland Browns, 12, 35
Cole, Larry, 5
Cotton Bowl, 26, 27
"Cradle of Quarterbacks, the" 28
Cross, Randy, 31

Dallas Cowboys
    Cole with, 5
    Staubach with, 19–22, **21**
    Super Bowls, 13, 43
DeBerg, Steve, 28, 35
Deford, Frank, 8
Deglau, Jim, 9–10
Denver Broncos
    Elway with, 32, 34–38, **37**
    Manning with, 39
    Super Bowl, 20
"Drive, the" 35–36

Elway, John Albert, Jr.
    AFC Championship Games, 35–36
    with Baltimore Colts, 34, **34**, 36
    basic facts about, 32–33, 39
    with Denver Broncos, 32, 34–38, **37**
    as high school football player, 32–33
    Manning and, 39
    NFL records, 35
    in Pro Football Hall of Fame, 38, **39**
    records set by, 33, 35, 38
    retirement of, 38
    at Stanford, 33–34, 35
    Super Bowls, 32, 36–38
"Elway cross, the" 35

15 and the Mahomies Foundation, 55
Forystek, Gary, 26
Fox Sports, 47

GOAT, the, 40, 45
Goshawks, 19, 20
Gradkowski, Bruce, 28
"Greatest Throw of All Time, the" 5
Green Bay Packers, 37

Hail Mary pass, first, 19
Hanratty, Terry, 26
Hardman, Mecole, 54
Heisman Trophy, 16, 17, 18
Henson, Drew, 42
Herrmann, Mark, 36
Hinton, Chris, 36
Hoobler, Marianne, 16
Hostetler, Jeff, 28
Hurts, Jalen, 32

Jackson, Lamar, 32
Johnny Unitas Stadium (Towson University), 11
Jurgensen, Sonny, 13

Kansas City Chiefs
    Mahomes with, 5–6, 48, 51–54, **52, 55**
    Montana with, 30–31
    Super Bowl loss by, 47
Kansas City Current, 51
Kelce, Travis, 48
Kelly, Jim, 28
Kingsbury, Kliff, 49, 50
Kiper, Mel, Jr., 40
Kostos, Nick, 7
Kush, Frank, 36

Landry, Tom, 23
Leahy, Frank, 9
Lewis, Ray, 45, 46
Lisch, Rusty, 26
Lombardi, Vince, 11
Los Angeles Rams, 53, 54

Madden, John, 44
Maguire, Paul, 37
Mahomes, Patrick
    AFC Championship Games, 48, 53, 54
    basic facts about, 49, 51, 55
    as high school football player, 49, **50**
    with Kansas City Chiefs, 5–6, 48, 51–54,
        52, 55
    as MVP, 49, 54
    records set by, 50, 52, 53, 54
    Super Bowls, 5–6, 48, 49, 53, 54
    with Texas Tech University, 49–51
Make-A-Wish Foundation, 31
Manning, Peyton, **6**
    Brady and, 43
    with Denver Broncos, 39
    as MVP, 4, 5, 43
    records set by, 4
    Super Bowls, 39, 43
Marino, Dan, 13, 28
Marshall, Leonard, 30

McCarthy, Jim, 17
Miami Dolphins, 20
Michigan Wolverines, 41–42, **42**
Miller, Von, 4
Montana, Joe
    AFC Championship Game, 31
    basic facts about, 25–26, 28, 31
    Brady and, 41
    injuries, 30
    with Kansas City Chiefs, 30–31
    nicknames, 25
    at Notre Dame, 26–27
    in Pro Football Hall of Fame, 25, 31
    records set by, 28
    retirement of, 31
    with San Francisco 49ers, 24, **27**, 27–30,
        30, 36
    Super Bowls, 28, 29, 30, **30**, 36
Morris, Eric, 51
Morton, Craig, 19, 20
Most Valuable Players (MVPs)
    Brady, 43, 44, 45
    Mahomes, 49, 54
    Manning, 4, 5, 43
    Staubach, 20
    Unitas, 10, 11, 12
M&T Bank Stadium (Baltimore), 11
Murray, Kyler, 32

Namath, Joe, 12–13, 28
National Football Conference (NFC)
    Championship Game (1982), 24
National Football League (NFL), 10–11
    See also Super Bowls
New England Patriots
    AFC Championship, 53
    Brady with, 40, 43–44, **44**
    Super Bowls, 41, 43
New Orleans Saints, 5
New York Giants, 10, 11, 30, 36
New York Jets, 12–13

Orange Bowl, 42

passing game, 6
Pearson, Drew, 19
Pennington, Chad, 42
Pennsylvania, western, and quarterbacks, 28
Peterson, Carl, 30–31
Philadelphia Eagles, 54
Pittsburgh Steelers
    Bradshaw with, 5
    Super Bowls, 43
    Unitas and, 9
Prescott, Dak, 23
Presidential Medal of Freedom, 16

Pro Bowl, 15
Pro Football Hall of Fame
Elway, 38, **39**
Montana, 25, 31
Namath, 28
Staubach, 23
Unitas, 13, 14
western Pennsylvanians in, 28
Pryor, Terrelle, 28

quarterbacks
dual-threat, 32
Hall of Fame, from western Pennsylvania,
28
qualities of best, 4–5, 6–7

Rawlings, Mike, **22**
Reeves, Dan, 34
Reid, Andy, 51–52
Rice, Jerry, 45, 46
Rodgers, Aaron, 46, 52

Sanders, Barry, 46
San Diego Chargers, 13
San Francisco 49ers
Montana with, 24, **27**, 27–30, **30**, 36
Super Bowls, 36, 43, 48
Sharpe, Shannon, 46
Shaw, George, 10
Sherman, Anthony, 55
Smith, Alex, 52
Sports Illustrated, 8, 14, 29
St. Louis Rams, 43–44
Stafford, Matthew, 53
Stars & Stripes (newspaper), 18
Staubach, Roger
basic facts about, 16–17
with Dallas Cowboys, 19–22, **21**
health of, 22
as Heisman Trophy winner, 16, 17, 18
as mental health–related causes speaker,
22–23, **22**
as MVP, 20
nicknames, 20
Presidential Medal of Freedom and, 16
in Pro Football Hall of Fame, 23
records set by, 20, 21, 29
retirement of, 21, **22**
Super Bowls, 17, 20
on switch to quarterback position, 17
in US Navy, 16, 17–19, **18**, 20
Super Bowls
Brady, 36, 40, 41, 43–44, **44**, 45–46, 47,
54
Elway, 32, 36–38
first, 10–11

first overtime in, 46
franchises with most wins, 43
Mahomes, 5–6, 48, 49, 53, 54
Manning, 39, 43
Montana, 28, 29, 30, **30**, 36
Staubach, 17, 20
Unitas, 12–13
Swann, Lynn, 5

Tagliabue, Paul, 15
Tampa Bay Buccaneers, 46–47, 54
Taylor, Nate, 51, 54
Tennessee Titans, 53
Texas Tech University Red Raiders, 49–51
Trubisky, Mitch, 51

Unitas, John Constantine, Johnny U, **12**
with Baltimore Colts, 8–13, **9**
basic facts about, 8–9
with Bloomfield Rams, 9
college football career, 9
death of, 11
footwear worn by, 15
injuries, 14, **14**
last public football pass by, 11
M&T Bank Stadium and, 11
as MVP, 10, 11, 12
NFL Championship Games, 10, 11
nickname, 13
Pittsburgh Steelers and, 9
Pro Bowl and, 15
in Pro Football Hall of Fame, 13, 14, 28
records set by, 10, 11
retirement of, 13
with San Diego Chargers, 13
as sportscaster, 13
in Super Bowls, 12–13
University of Alabama, 42
University of Houston, 26
University of Louisville (Kentucky), 9
University of Notre Dame, 26–27
University of Pittsburgh, 9
University of Texas, 26
US Navy, 16, 17–19, **18**, 20

Vinatieri, Adam, 44

Walsh, Bill, 27–28
Watson, DeShaun, 51
Wersching, Ray, 24
White, Randy, 21
Wyche, Sam, 25

Young, Steve, 29, 30

Zimmerman, Paul, 29

PICTURE CREDITS

Cover: Steve Jacobson/Shutterstock
 6: Zuma Press, Inc./Alamy Stock Photo
 9: RLFE Pix/Alamy Stock Photo
12: Associated Press
14: Associated Press
18: Cliff Welch/Icon SMI 357/Cliff Welch/Icon SMI/Newscom
21: MBRA-Ai Wire/"Ai Wire Photo Service"/Newscom
22: Fitzcrittle/Shutterstock
27: Al Bolub/ZUMA Press/Newscom
30: Joseph W. McDonough/Icon SMI 500/John W.
    McDonough/Icon SMI/Newscom
34: Associated Press
37: Ben Munn/Cal Sport Media/Newscom
39: Associated Press
42: Associated Press
44: UPI/Alamy Stock Photo
46: Julien's Auctions/MEGA/Newscom/CJMAR/Newscom
50: Associated Press
52: Rich Graessle/Icon Sportswire CGV/Rich Graessle/Icon
    Sportswire/Newscom
55: Scott Winters/Icon Sportswire DGM/Scott Winters/Icon
    Sportswire/Newscom

ABOUT THE AUTHOR

After graduating from the University of Oregon, James Roland became a newspaper reporter, primarily focused on education. He later became a magazine writer and editor as well as an author of more than a dozen books. He and his wife, Heidi, have three children, Chris, Alexa, and Carson.